the women who hate ME.

POETRY
1980-1990

Also by Dorothy Allison

Trash

the women who hate ME.

POETRY
1980-1990

DOROTHY ALLISON

Firebrand Books
Ithaca, New York

The original version of *The Women Who Hate Me* was published in 1983 by Long Haul Press.

Book and cover design by Betsy Bayley
Typesetting by Bets Ltd.

Printed in the United States on acid-free paper by McNaughton & Gunn

Library of Congress Card No. 91–311

acknowledgments

Janis Kelly, Nancy Bereano, Joy Johannessen, and Alix Layman gave me time with my mother before she died. For both of us—mama and me—no other gift was ever so important.

for mama

contents

dumpling girl/9
upcountry/10
mattie lee gibson/19
the women who hate me/21
silence grew between us/32
to the bone/33
liar/34
tomato song/36
hollow-cheeked/38
when i drink i become the joy of faggots/39
not speaking/screaming/42
butter my tongue/43
we all nourish truth with our tongues/45
the terror of my enemies/48
a woman like an ocean/49
appetite/51
she plays it tight/52
what is the dream of flesh?/53
boston, massachusetts/55
little enough/58
all those imaginary ladies/60
whoring away my imagination/62
i chose this ground/63
reason enough to love you/65
the women who love me/66
we make love/67
the other side of the wall/68

dumpling child

A southern dumpling child
  biscuit eater, tea sipper
  okra slicer, gravy dipper,
I fry my potatoes with onions
  stew my greens with pork

And ride my lover high up
on the butterfat shine of her thighs
where her belly arches and sweetly tastes
of rock salt on watermelon
sunshine sharp teeth bite light
and lick slow like mama's
favorite dumpling child.

upcountry

1.

The summer you were seven
and I was nine, I knew it all
the light in your eyes
the darkness in mine
little sister, did I tell you then
what I never said after
how much I loved you
how certain I was it wouldn't help?

The fire you set that I lied about
the glass I broke, you pressed to your mouth,
that red brick porch and slanting yard
a dirt stretch of dead grass and abandoned cars
the country of all my dreams, night terrors
where your eyes were always growing dull
and someone was always screaming

the country where we knew
ourselves
despised.

When the uncles came to visit
pickups parked aslant the yard
bottles that rocked from board to rim
shotguns point-down beside the gears
a leather holster or canvas sling
I watched the neighbors squint their eyes
no-count, low down, disgusting,
I put my nails to the bones of my neck
squeezed, trying to understand.

You don't know where she's been.
I know where I've been.

2.

Upcountry, a woman lived
in the crack of two mountains
your daddy's mama growing tomato, okra, beans
a house with two rooms, a central hall,
a porch where the boards bred crickets.

Oh, to run away for that creek,
the sun, her eyes, to carry water
up from that spring, work her garden
die at eleven, lockjaw taken
from a nail on that porch.

Your daddy's mama, I wanted her for mine
the way she sometimes looked at you
seeing her son in the set of your shoulders
nothing of me
bitchwhelp, mama's older daughter
mouth like a knifeblade, cut deep, angry
eyes like the glint on a shotgun sight
dark enough to prove the old tale true
Bastard
marked by the spit of the devil.

Upcountry
I wanted to go upcountry
trade you for your grandmother
trade for that porch, silence
the mountain, the weed-dye blankets
as far from the low country
as sin from saintly.
I could be saintly easy enough.

You always said
women don't make babies
with women.

3.

It's old terribly old
this grief between us
speaks another language
metal crisp against the teeth
coins that crack the molars
spit blood, bone, and memory.

Do you remember the screaming?
The bushes where you hid
our stepfather running after us
caught me more often than you
ran blood down my body?

Do you remember that porch?
How I fell back onto the corner
cut deep between my legs
screamed for mama driving up
catching my scream in the pit of her fear
  my blood in her hands
  my hands between my legs
  the scream dying in my throat
  strangling on the certainty
  I would die.

Bleeding across the car seat
mutely pushing at the blood
I knew it would ruin the seatcover
mama's uniform, your white curls.
I knew they'd have to cut away, throw out
the seatcover, your hair, my body.

Maybe it was not then
I learned to hate doctors
might have been sooner
but the way they laughed was enough
the jokes I wasn't supposed
to understand.

Eight years old, and fucking a post—
hard up for it, can't you imagine?

I imagined my body
widened into a mountain creek
flooded the countryside with my dying.
I did not want to wake to pain
sweat burning the stitches between
one leg pinned, the other leg wide.

When you came in
your hair cut short
I screamed, hoarse as a crow
YOU, YOU, YOU, YOU
how I loved you.

Mad months lying pinned and silent
tears and sweat running
my open mouth, my cheek, your hand
lifting the blanket
to see what I couldn't.

Time made me walk like an old woman
bent, stiff, tight
with the laughter on the street
the boys saying
Let me. You won't even notice.
I'll use the hole you made.

4.

But it was you   you who turned
  quick to fuck them
  quick to beg them
  to hold you closer
  make you safer
  ripen the valley between your legs
  and be just once
  soft and filling
  as buttermilk bubbles
  in a baby's mouth.

I shouted, called you whore
but dreamed of your laughter
justice ripening a baby at
the back of my tongue.

Pink little sister, blue-eyed,
stupid girl, family pet
eyes of glass that nothing lived behind
How I
hated you, loved you, wanted you
to melt into my bones
pass to me the honey of how
they looked at you.
Rot-sweet, dull-eyed sister
took to fucking like I took to silence.

5.

Years later you gave me
an envelope of dried blood, hair
a memory of that house, that porch.
I gave you a knife, a handle I carved
beanwire edging hammered nailheads
that I meant to mean me and you.

I meant it to edge
the memories never acknowledged
dreams not shared, the metal keen
coin-hammered, hard.
I meant it to make a piece of caring
cut the lump of all we've swallowed
the hatred we have resisted
the love we pretend
never made any difference.

mattie lee gibson

A cedar chest of lace and linen
she would not wear underwear
though she kept it in stacks
we were not to touch.
The money my mama gave her for food
went on silk, lace, thin satin briefs
layered with vanilla in a deep old chest
while she went naked under print dresses
and we ate peaches four days out of five.

Her teeth were brown, heavy in her mouth.
I watched the rolls of muscle in her neck
under her loose stained skin, those teeth,
her twisted fingers, wide legs and the touch
of brown on her lips, the thick wad of snuff
rolling forward and back.

Okra, strawberries, sweet-eared white corn
my sister five and I seven
she sent us up the clay road
blind side of the property
with a brown paper sack.
I cut my knees on wire fences
sister grew a terror of snakes
while granny told mama we were so beautiful
farmers paid us tribute on our walks.

Granny gathered blackberries, stripped muscadine vines
stepped wide over ditches and peed straight down
called me *dark angel* and sister *mama's golden child*
while hinting at things mama wouldn't explain.
Her sons took to liquor, her daughters made babies.
Eleven children out of her body and only eight survived
but never a baby blanket tainted the smell of cedar
no hot cotton sun smell, no sweat, snuff, or piss.

How can you hate someone you love so?
Some old woman peeing in a ditch
some old woman flesh of my flesh
some old woman, rough, hard, dreaming
linen pale as birch heart, satin pale as death.

I don't know who got it
her cedar chest, her linen and vanilla,
none of it worn, none of it stained.

Only know they sold it
put her naked in that box
walnut   brass
a lining of much-desired silk.

the women who hate me

1.

The women who do not know me.

The women who, not knowing me, hate me
mark my life, rise in my dreams and shake their loose hair
throw out their thin wrists, narrow their already sharp eyes
say   *Who do you think you are?*

Lazy, useless, cuntsucking, scared, stupid
What you scared of anyway?
Their eyes, their hands, their voices.
Terrifying.

The women who hate me cut me
as men can't.   Men don't count.
I can handle men. Never expected better
of any man   anyway.
                                        But the women,
shallow-cheeked young girls the world was made for
safe little girls who think nothing of bravado
who never got over by playing it tough.

What do they know of my fear?

What do they know of the women in my body?
My weakening hips, sharp good teeth,
angry nightmares, scarred cheeks,
fat thighs, fat everything.

Don't smile too wide. You look like a fool.
Don't want too much. You an't gonna get it.

An't gonna get it.
Goddamn.

Say goddamn and kick somebody's ass
that I am not even half what I should be,
full of terrified angry bravado.

BRAVADO.
The women who hate me
don't know
can't imagine
life-saving, precious bravado.

2.

God on their right shoulder
righteousness on their left,
the women who hate me never use words
like hate   speak instead of nature
of the spirit not housed in the flesh
as if my body, a temple of sin,
didn't mirror their own.

Their measured careful words echo
earlier coarser stuff   say

What do you think you're doing?
Who do you think you are?

Whitetrash
no-count
bastard
mean-eyed
garbage-mouth
cuntsucker
cuntsucker
no good to anybody, never did diddlyshit anyway.

You figured out yet who you an't gonna be?

The women who hate me hate
their insistent desires, their fat lusts
swallowed and hidden, disciplined to nothing
narrowed to bone and dry hot dreams.
The women who hate me deny
hunger and appetite,
the cream delight
of a scream
that arches the thighs and fills
the mouth with singing.

3.

Something hides here
a secret thing shameful and complicated.
Something hides in a tight mouth
a life too easily rendered
a childhood of inappropriate longing
a girl's desire to grow into a man
a boyish desire to stretch and sweat.

Every three years I discover again
that no, I knew nothing before.
Everything must be dragged out,
looked over again. The unexamined life
is the lie, but still
must I every time deny
everything I knew before?

4.

My older sister tells me flatly
she don't care who I take to my bed
what I do there.   Tells me finally
she sees no difference between
her husbands, my lovers. Behind it all
we are too much the same to deny.

My little sister thinks my older crazy
thinks me sick
more shameful to be queer than crazy
as if her years hustling ass,
her pitiful junky whiteboy
saved through methadone and marriage, all that
asslicking interspersed with asskicking,
all those pragmatic family skills we share mean nothing
measured against the little difference
of who and what I am.

My little sister   too
is one of the women who hate me.

5.

I measure it differently, what's shared,
what's denied, what no one wants recognized.

My first lover's skill at mystery,
how one day she was there, the next gone;
the woman with whom I lived for eight years
but slept with less than one;
the lover who tied me to the foot of her bed
when I didn't really want that
but didn't really know
what else I could get.

What else can I get?
Must I rewrite my life
edit it down to a parable where everything
turns out for the best?

But then what would I do with the lovers
too powerful to disappear   the women
too hard to melt to soft stuff?
Now that I know that soft stuff
was never where I wanted to put my hand.

6.

The women who hate me
hate   too   my older sister
with her many children, her weakness for
good whiskey, country music, bad men.
She says the thing *women's lib* has given her
is a sense she don't have to stay too long
though she does
still she does
much too long.

7.

I am not so sure anymore of the difference.
I do not believe anymore in the natural superiority
of the lesbian, the difference between my sisters and me.

Fact is, for all I tell my sisters
I turned out terrific at it myself:
sucking cunt, stroking ego, provoking,
manipulating, comforting, keeping.
Plotting my life around mothering
other women's desperation
the way my sisters
build their lives
around their men.
Till I found myself   sitting at the kitchen table
shattered glass, blood in my lap and her
the good one with her stern insistence
just standing there wanting me
to explain it to her   save her from being
alone with herself.

Or that other one
another baby-butch wounded girl
    How can any of us forget how wounded
    any of us have to be to get that hard?
Never to forget that working class says nothing
does not say who she was   how she was
fucking me helpless. Her hand on my arm
raising lust to my throat   that lust
everyone says does not happen
though it goes on happening
all the time.

How can I speak of her, us together?
Her touch drawing heat from my crotch to my face
her face, terrifying, wonderful.
Me saying, "Yeah, goddamn it, yeah,
put it to me, ease me, fuck me, anything. . ."
till the one thing I refused
then back up against a wall
her rage ugly in the muscles of her neck
her fist swinging up to make a wind
a wind blowing back to my mama's cheek
past my stepfather's arm.

I ask myself over and over how I
came to be standing in such a wind?
How I came to be held up like my mama
with my jeans, my shoes locked in a drawer
and the woman I loved breathing on me,
    "You bitch.   You damned fool."

    "You want to try it?"
    "You want to walk to Brooklyn
      barefooted?"
    "You want to try it
      mothernaked?"

Which meant   of course   I had to decide
how naked   I was willing to go   where.

Do I forget all that?
Deny all that?
Pretend I am not
my mama's daughter
my sister's mirror?
Pretend I have not
at least as much lust
in my life   as pain?

Where   then   will I find the country
where women never wrong women
where we will sit knee to knee
finally listening
to the whole
naked truth
of our lives?

silence grew between us

When you touched me
my womb filled with light
my mouth   with light
the deep places between my breasts
flooded light full of the smell
of baking eggplant, pure desire.

But the summer was a stone
grinding in our mouths
a rock between our legs
blocking touch   sensation   or even
the hope of consummation.

My fingers grew webs of iron
my hands on your body felt
numbed and cold. You shivered.
I sweated, cried, screamed.
We cried all summer.

"Hold me," I begged,
but your fingers too were iron.
"Rock me," you pleaded,
but my fingers would not move
for the shame, the fear that stopped
our hands   our mouths.

Silence grew between us
like a blackened stillborn egg
still swelling.

to the bone

That summer I did not go crazy,
spoke every day to my mama who insisted
our people do not go crazy.
We make instead that sudden evening
silence that follows the shotgun blast.
We stand up alone twenty years after
like a scarecrow in a field
pie-eyed, toothless, naming
our enemies and outliving them.
That summer I talked to death
like an old friend, a husky voice
whispering up from my cunt, echoing
around my knees, laughing.
That summer I did not go crazy
but I wore
            very close
very close
            to the bone.

liar

I still cannot believe it
how they lie, how they turn
their eyes out to the light
   square forward
set their mouths,
   smile wet, shiny-toothed.
As calmly as speaking the truth
   they lie.

I pull papers out of my pockets.
"Here, you said it here. Look here."
But the cameras are turning,
   six minutes gone, no more.
The reporters wrap it up
   and I am left with the papers
the flat proof of a truth
   no one takes seriously.

I had not heard that truth had died
bleeding from a thousand papercut silences
strangled on the bones of a lie
put out loud enough and long
   a lie that swelled meat on a diet of whispers
   a lie that grew wings brown and substantial
   as plainly made as dirt or cabbages
   trustworthy as syphilis or plague.

Oh liar!
Will you talk to me?
Will you sit at my table,
  eat my gravy,
  slide over and grin into my mouth
  the mouth I'll keep wide for you?
Oh liar,
Will you fuck me?
Will you slide your cabbage hands over my belly
your dirty mouth up my thigh?

Oh liar, liar!
Is this how you did it?
Turned truth around and stuck her
hard on the angle of your desire?

Did I mistake your sex, your intention?

No matter, liar, come on my tongue
salt gush in my mouth. Sex an't the motive
and I've a surprise for you.

Six minutes is more than enough.
Six minutes will root you deep
where the heat, the razors wait.
No lights, no cameras, no audience to please
just truth   and me   and patience.

I'm gonna harvest you a little at a time.

tomato song

I'm gonna give up my last name
  and maybe my first
call myself Nite's daughter or Pusskicka
  or something really crude
  full of fucks and thrusting gestures.

I'm going to grow a rage like a tomato,
kind of a great red fruit could
wreck bridges or bring down sauce
on half the city
tell low-down jokes
proposition old ladies
lick their cheeks, offer to
climb up under their skirts
for free.

Might as well live up to my reputation.
Might as well play the movie out
roll my tomato up Broadway
knock people over
from half a block further
than Brooklyn,
move to Canarsie,
buy a shotgun.

Throw parties? Hell,
I might as well throw parties.
Anybody here want to go to a party?
You're gonna have to dress for it
might make a movie of it,
put you all in the Tomato epic,
premiere it on Times Square.

No apologies, explanations, excuses,
nothing but me, my tomato, my rages,
  my name,
  my name.

hollow-cheeked

I want to be a hollow-cheeked woman of mystery
coming down the street
in my black clothes and grey vest
the outlaw lover
long-haired lesbian
mythical bitch.

Want them to tell my stories in
Tallahassee
Amherst
Washington, D.C.
and
New York City.

Such a legend I would make
lean, fast, and
largely unknown
but mysterious
fascinating
always provocative
hollow-cheeked
which is the first problem.

Did you ever notice how the famous ones
are always thin?

I could be thin.
I could be very good at leanness
if you did not taste so good
so good with chocolate, so good with gravy
so filling, the legend, you, my appetite
rich, delicious, mesmerizing
like fine sherry with a sharp edge
or attitude with tight pants.

when i drink i become the joy of faggots

When I drink I become
                                        the joy of faggots.
I try not to drink too often.
When I was younger I couldn't drink at all.

I have grown into this joy
this sense that the night is full of possibilities
conversation an art that can be perfected
with gesture and ease and a glass in the hand.

When I was young I said I would be a writer
   with no sense what it could mean
   how hard it would be.
My friends talked sympathetically
of another friend from Texas
who had driven to Florida in an antique car
who was known for how charmingly he could weep.

A Writer, a Poet, he would drink and talk to me
of how all the men at school wanted to fuck him
of his desire to leave them at the pavement edge
knowing they would remember and want always
his car   his tears   his ass   his poems.

Sensitive,
everyone was sure he was sensitive.
He told me how when his roommate stood
silent over his bed
he reached up, slapped him,
slapped him again.

He wanted me, you know.
I knew.

His roommate used to talk of how he resisted it,
the desire, the burn for a beautiful boy.
A scholar of greek and latin and buggery
when he drank he became foolish
his moustache hanging damp.

I wanted him, you know.
I knew.

In the middle of the night I dream
old friends and lechery.
Since I do not drink, I burn.
Is this what everybody knew that I didn't?
How desire and denial roll in the glass?
How the fire, the fire consumes?

She had hands with fingers like tapers
lean legs, dark hair, a car.
Everywhere I saw that car
just the briefest flash of her
hair, legs, fingers   and gone.
Sensitive,
God, she knew she was sensitive.
And when I stood over her
she slapped me with the delight of a boy.

I wanted her, you know.
They knew.

Their poems were published everywhere.
I made a small fire of mine on the beach.

There is a small fire in a glass of whiskey
a backfire that counters the fire inside
like the fire in the eyes of an angry woman
who suspects that inside her hides a faggot
standing silent over someone's bed
holding still for the blows the sensitive give.

not speaking/screaming

Silence is *the* problem,
she said.   She insisted.
I went for a walk in the grey morning
up Seventh Avenue toward the park
with the pigeons and the Boarshead delivery men.
On every block someone camped,
some mottled grey face shivered
settled in a bed of trash.

Have you noticed the sudden increase
in shoeshine stands? I asked her.
She kept her hands in her pockets,
her chin fierce.   No.
I pulled my silence in around me,
remembered years disappearing
because I would not speak of them.
You're right, of course, I told her,
gave in   fell silent
thinking still of that tall woman
who walks Broadway with such long steps
and screams
and screams.

butter my tongue

Butter, butter, butter my tongue.
I've lost my rhythm
the pulse of my language
feel ready to break
feel ready to crumble
feel ready to fall
like a doll without knees.

I was meant for a gospel singer
sipping whiskey or bourbon
behind the stage
going out to croon *Sweet Jesus*
(breathe) *Oh hold me up,*
Hold me up in the air.

I was meant for Moses and meat
and sweet gospel juice in the seat,
rising higher, higher.
I had lyric in my belly
wind in my mouth, fear and desire
rising higher, higher,
screaming low against the dark
throwing-back rhythm
from the windows of a '57 chevy
the year I was eight
before I lost rhythm, language, and soul
curled down around my own tongue
swallowed my people, my history
and wrapped myself
in a clipped language
never rose to any height.

Butter, butter, butter my tongue
and give me back
all I have lost.

we all nourish truth with our tongues

1.

I am saying that the world is wider
than anyone thought   the women
far more important   their true voices,
the real events of their lives
not cleaned up   not lied about
stark   dirty   and hard.

We all nourish truth with our tongues
not in sour-batter words that never take shape
nor line-driven stories bent to skirt the edge
of our great exhaustion, desire, and doubt.
We all use simply the words of our own lives
to say what we really want
to lie spent on our lovers
put teeth to all we hate
to strain the juice of our history
between what has been allowed
and what has always been denied,
the active desire to take hold of the root.

The root is choice.
It will not grow in a box
  a barred room walled round
  by those who shout
  the same old words
  over and over.
I am saying that the root of fear
  is choice.
The root of all desire:
  choice.

2.

In the dirt country where I was born
the words that named me were so terrible
no one would speak them
so always just over my head
a silent language damned me.

I learned then that what no one would say
was the thing about which nothing could be done.
If they would not say *Lesbian*
I could not say pride.
If they would not say *Queer*
I could not say courage.
If they would not name me
Bastard, worthless, stupid, whore
I could not grab onto my own spoken language,
my love for my kind, myself.

I learned there is only one language
and it either speaks truly or lies.
But sometimes it must go on a long time
before the whole truth comes out
and until that moment all the words
are lies. Still I tell you
there is only one language.

What I am saying is the words
are growing in my mouth.
All the names of god will be spoken,
all the hidden secret things made known.
We will root in dirt our mothers watered
sing songs, tell stories echoed in their mouths.

Then with no walls around us, you and I
will speak of truth to each other,
the soil that grows the vegetable
as deeply as the flower that never
touches the soil.

the terror of my enemies

The act of love as I dream it
is distinct from the act
my enemies imagine.
How can I display
the tenderness with which
we enfold
I and the army
I invite to my bed,
the hard-hipped aching women
I put my tongue,
my hands to,
the women whose hands
widen and fill me,
whose tongues suck salt
to the surface
of my skin.

The act of murder as I dream it
is distinct from the terror
of my enemies.
They cannot imagine
the bone speed of my rage,
the strawberry sweetness
of my revenge
measured cold
and bitter sharp
behind my tongue,
the regard of these
slow eyes.

a woman like an ocean

All last spring I imagined
falling in love with the ocean
going down at midnight, dawn, sunset
to kneel and worship a female movement
slow jewel drops running forward and back.

In the city I have to take the D train
out to Coney Island, Brighton Beach
walk the rock slope, rotted boardwalk.
It is the same ocean, has to be,
but not to be fallen in love with.

Greaseshine, weed-lined, trash high.
No one swims, no one my age.
Drunken boys throw each other forward
come up glistening, cursing.
It has to be the same ocean.
Has to be, can't be
cannot be loved like the other.

On Brant Beach I knew her   a suburban ocean
like a girl in a well-tailored suit.
Clean. Watched over. Protected.
Walking a line toward the horizon every day.
When after three weeks the storm came
we went down to watch her roll over and scream.
Foam gathered grease
layered yellow and cold.
Sunset brought in a dark wind.
A chill went up my back
like lust.

I have never been able to resist her
the muscles of a strong woman who laughs
her hands rough as she rolls me over
talks mean, drags me forward and back,
when she fucks like an ocean, a bruiser
makes shell-puckered hickey-bite marks,
when she moves like she's breaking out thunder,
when she rises like spray in the wind.
Singing roll over, roll over and ride me
roll over, swim down, laugh out loud.

Those last days the ocean became her.
Roaring dark, strong, salt stinging like sweat
called my name till my teeth ached, tongue trembled
rolled foam heat right down to my knees.

appetite

It must sound better than it is
the women who go to France for the summer
a spiced croissant smeared with yellow butter
cream in the coffee. I grow fat
in Brooklyn.

In Brooklyn
another woman makes herself lean
a season in the belly has turned
and her lust is all pomegranate juice,
shredded carrots, grapefruit shipped in
from Florida.

From Florida
my mama writes that the custody
fight goes well though she almost lost her job
when the in-laws, lying, called her dirty, brought
in the health inspector from
the state.

The state
sits on my appetites, will not let
any of us travel to France, or Florida easily.
The work goes on hungry or starving for hope—
a pomegranate swollen red rage in
my life.

she plays it tight

A woman I love
really thinks she can
make of herself
a boy
a lean-hipped
hard-eyed
cold-hearted
piece of
rough trade.
She plays it tight
to her knucklebones
her line of
hip to knee
to dark-edged
turn and knuckle
under.
She is the only boy
in a girl body
west of Hudson
never notices how
the girls in boy bodies
mock her moves
hate her
for what she
doesn't value
the girl body
starved to
boy.

what is the dream of flesh?

Never enough
never good enough
I fail to be what is most needed
cannot even imagine
a separate place for my own needs
fears   desires.

The dream of the flesh is enough
of the spirit enough
of the brain enough
not too much
not an unjust demand
or a greedy one.
The flesh is hungry
for just enough
milk to the rim of the glass
a kiss that rests fully on the mouth
time that goes steadily
does not run out screaming
Come on.   *Come on!*

Flesh on flesh
sunlight on my eyelids
I dream the dream of the body
the muscles that long to loosen
the belly's cry for justice
bean soup and quiet for the eating
a breath that rises easy
to the mouth.

I will not give one for the other
trade flesh for mind or memory.
The dream of flesh is integrity
the body joined with its own ambitions
honestly acknowledging the cunt
as fully as the belly,
honestly honoring the women
who stir my flesh to dream.

boston, massachusetts

Boston, Massachusetts, many years ago
a woman told me   about a woman dead
a woman who might   not have been known
to be   a lesbian.

No one is sure they knew that.
The cops didn't say that, they said
she was wearing a leather jacket, blue jeans, worn boots,
had dark cropped hair and was new to the neighborhood,
living in an old brick rowhouse with three other women.
Said she was carrying a can of gasoline.
They did not say why,
a car waiting,
a jar of sticky brushes.
Said she was white
her friends were white
the neighborhood was bad
she and her friends were fools
didn't belong there.
Were queer anyway.
Said the young rough crowd of men
laughed a lot
when they stopped her,
that she laughed back,
and then
they made her pour the gasoline
over her head.

Later, some cop said
she was a hell of a tough bitch
'cause she walked two blocks on her own feet,
two blocks to the all-night grocery
where another little crowd watched
going
Shiiiiiiit!
Will you look at that?
Look at that!

I read about it in the paper—two paragraphs.
I have carried that story with me ever since
wanting more, wanting no one to have to be
those two stark paragraphs.

We become our deaths.
Our names disappear and our lovers leave town,
heartbroken, crazy,
but we are the ones who die.
We are the forgotten
burning in the streets
hands out, screaming,
This is not all I am.
I had something else in mind to do.
Not on that street,
always and only that
when there was so much more she had to do.

Sometimes
when I love my lover
I taste in my mouth

ashes
gritty
grainy

grating between the teeth
the teeth of a woman
unquestionably known
to be a lesbian.

little enough

On President Street a lady standing in her yard
reminded me of every aunt I ever met, stiff-backed
and tired but laughing in a rough loud voice.
"You ever see such ugly furniture?" Everything for
sale: a chest, table, counter and chairs, bent lamps
and broken cabinets. "But the way things are, if it
stands still, I'd sell it." She laughed and I
could not leave, for hope she'd laugh again.
"You girls out walking on such a pretty day,
why don't you just buy me out and let me go in?
You look at this stuff. This an't bad stuff.
Ugly but strong like they say, and clean, clean."
Which it was—scrubbed up and polished, oiled shiny
in the sunlight, like that lady and her concrete yard.

"You girls," she smiled at us, invited us in to
see her new kitchen, the furniture set aside,
the walls redone. "I've lived here twenty years,
worked forty for the city. You got to work, you know
even when the body wants no part of it. You got to work."
I know. I have always known. I smiled at her and
memorized her address, watched the light at her
temples, the tight hair lightening with age,
her hands swinging a spray bottle of polish and
a flat yellow cotton rag. *I know. I know.*
I praised her walls, her cabinets, hugged to myself
her forty years of stubborn work, survival.

The women I dream of loving take care of themselves,
their people, put up shelves in the evening,
boil off chicken stock before bed, sleep hard and
are up again before dawn for the quiet, the hope of
a few good lines, another little piece of a story.
Like her, that old woman on President Street, as sturdy
as her pine cabinets and hand-scraped doors. "You girls,"
she said, and I knew then why she'd stopped us, what
she'd seen in how my lover touched my neck, knew that
none of us would say the word, say *lesbian* or even *lovers.*

We would talk instead of houses, kitchens,
furniture, and how it is, making your own way in a
world where nobody's handing out anything for free,
of soup recipes and bean dishes rescued from burning pots.
"God an't gonna reach down and smooth things," she laughed.
"God's got enough on his mind." She waved her hand as if
to say God's got little enough to do with us.
"But you can do it. Get yourself a piece of
something important to you and work it, work it
with time and effort and care." In the code
we were speaking, I could not tell if she meant
the house
or life
or love.

all those imaginary ladies

She asked me,
How many lovers have you had?
Isn't it strange how tacky that question makes me?

I promise you
I was not a pursuer, not a seducer.
I have always been surprised by passion
and its death. But I made a mistake in the beginning
told a lie that confused all that followed
said,
You are not the first.
said,
I know what I'm doing.

It was so frightening to be the lesbian between us,
to be that young and that certain
with her looking back at me, just as scared.
One of us had to be experienced.
One of us had to be responsible.

So I reassured her
invented women out of stories
adventures, anecdotes to tease her
while my fingers slipped up her hips
in holy helpless passion   and she
she laughed   relaxed   and loved me.

Ah, but the lie,
that lie has followed me
as if the women I spoke of
  trailed off in lines of flesh
  from my shaky fingers,
  trailed off and ran around
  telling their own stories
  of how I'd been
  and what we'd done.

All those imaginary ladies
told their own lies,
said,
  You are not the first.
said,
  Don't be afraid.
  Let me tell you about the first
  her   me   Dorothy.

Somewhere, someone is lying.
  is saying my name,
  is laughing
  is saying,

Shit, honey!
she pretended,
and I knew it
all the time.

whoring away my imagination

Mama wants me rich and famous.
An old lover keeps asking me when the hell
am I going to write that bestseller anyway?
I shrug. She has read so much of my work,
still never understands how the work
has its own rhythm, its own needs, how
sometimes I swear I'm transcribing, living
my life around the work not through it.
That other lover, the one followed me all those weeks
threatening to deliver me just the adventure I deserved,
she's saved all my letters, stories, poems,
plans on being famous shortly after me,
which is almost as funny as the one who wanted
me to pay her not to send the same stuff
to my boss.   So send it, I said.

Sitting down over work never seems
to get finished, head nodding exhausted
after eight hours of other people's typing,
typing my own journal-poems, short stories,
and those three novels never come to an end,
I pick up speed going nowhere
trying to hang onto the wider view
my life   the country
seen from the air.

i chose this ground

I chose this ground
New York City in the coldest decade
a lifetime away from the cornbread
warm milk hunger of my childhood.
I chose this ground
this lesbian city ripe with color
and fear, violence and hope,
languages, ambition and desire.
This ground rocking beneath my feet
quicksand or shale slope
gonna slip me into the river
drown me, like I never chose this ground
never fled the sucking mud
of a ground no one could hold,
women who lied to you, a region
where I wasn't supposed to exist,
where they say there are no black lesbians,
no poor white southerners who resist
being what everybody else thinks they are,
no women who write to survive, for hope
of a people set free, a city remade.
The ground swept clean.

Every Wednesday, every Sunday of her life
my grandma swept her yard, raked
the dust into smooth clean lines
the red dust that choked babies
and stained the boards of her porch.
She paid whatever rent was demanded
for the right to rake her yard
and when they put her out
three years before she died,
the uncles moved her to a yard
where the rocks had never been cleared

where glass and wire scraps threatened
our feet. She ignored the boxes sitting full,
went out to rake that ground
to clear herself a sense of place.
"Hold your ground," she told me.
I hold what I can be sure of—the
ground I have chosen—
New York City in the coldest decade.

reason enough to love you

The night my mama called—a Thursday night—
which meant, certainly, something was wrong,
you took my hand, sitting there on the bed
not interrupting while she told jokes and
I laughed and I told jokes and she laughed,
both of us trying to cry so soft, maybe
the other one could pretend not to hear.
You took my hand and held on tight while
my tears ran down your shoulder and mama
told another joke in my left ear.
You didn't make me explain, just held me
and took away some of the fear of dying.

The day they were shouting my name,
everyone looking at me like I was crazy
or had forgotten somehow to dress right
like all those nightmares from my childhood
you put your hand on my neck and squeezed
stayed close to me stayed close
and put your fear in another place.

And that morning when I woke up crying
not able to say why, it could have been anything,
any of ten good reasons to just lay back and cry,
you slid over and put your whole body over mine
gently, your hand in my hair, your mouth on my ear,
wrapping silence and love and the muscles of your thighs
all around me and let me cry let me cry
like no one ever let me before.

the women who love me

She could not sleep.
I could not stay awake.
She hinted that if I did not
I might wake up on the fire escape,
naked, on the roof or sidewalk.

I nodded, nodded, nodded out.

The women who love me
hold me when I sleep,
put their legs between mine.
Their fingers lace my cold ears.
They breathe on me, careful
not to wake me too soon.

The women who love me have
their own sisters to reconcile,
brothers, family and Broadway winds.
The women whose hands never touch my own
still reach me   turning round
to face their fear   laughing
at a hatred never meant to be understood.

They bank the ground I stand on
every time they stand against the wind
refuse to deny themselves, their people,
bend but do not fall,
hold to time
and steady struggle,
the reach of daylight,
the hope of women who love each other,
women who truly love each other.

we make love

We make love
and its a game called
Maybe you'll live long enough.

We make love
it's a game
it's a game called
I know what you want
but I'm not gonna give it.

We make love
we make love
it's a game
called
Just what you deserve
called
Justice
called
Despair.

It's a game
it's a game
called
The most vicious revenge
or
Reparations.

We make love
we make love
it's a game
it's a game

Even so
I come.

the other side of the wall

The other side of the wall they are making love
my mama croons a deep-throated bird under wet leaves,
rides my stepfather's staggered engine roar.
My sisters' eyes are inches from my ears.
The wall is kitchen-curtain thin.
Hear them? *Listen.*
This is why she married him.
Underneath, it is always sex.

My sisters' eyes are bicycle wheels.
Their fingers are wet, hot, hard.
Listen to them. The pump
of fingers, cock, and tongue.
Listen to my sisters breathing
every night, lips to my ears,
every night, after the bath and the shouting
he takes her to bed, grounds her
to the wall where our fingers
press the mystery, the unseen
clearly heard train of desire.

This side of the wall we are making love
teeth, tongue, hands all entwined.
You ride hard the edge of my hip, swing
me belly tight up to the flat of the wall.
I reach back, become a train gaining speed.
Just there I hear my sisters, breathing hard
their fingers sliding, wide as their eyes.
Listen. Just listen to us.
I could, I swear to you, be my mama.
You do, I swear, fuck like a man.

Only a little harder, and I'll break through.
My fingers will claw a hole.
This wall will come down.
We'll reach my sisters' straining fingers.
My eyes will fly up like a bird clearing ground
and that old grating mysterious engine
will shudder, and pound, and lift us all clear.